The Power of Managing Your Stress

15 Steps To Reduce Stress and Increase Health and Take Your Life Into Your Hands to Become a Happy, Healthy Person.

When you recognize that you are starting to stress out it's time to do something to counteract it – to manage your stress.

Stress can have serious impacts on your health, job, relationships, family and life in general. It isn't something to wait to correct.

Questions people ask:

- How do I realize that I am stressed?
- What can I do about it?
- How can I avoid it?

If you are looking for important information about managing stress pick up this important little book today.

Your Amazing Itty Bitty® Stress Reduction Book

15 Key Steps to Reduce Stress and Increase Health

Denise Thomson, CHC

Published by Itty Bitty® Publishing
A subsidiary of S & P Productions, Inc.

Copyright © 2018 **Denise Thomson**

All rights reserved. No part of this book may be reproduced or transmitted in any form or by any means, electronic or mechanical, including photocopying, recording or by any information storage and retrieval system, without written permission of the publisher, except for inclusion of brief quotations in a review.

Printed in the United States of America

Itty Bitty® Publishing
311 Main Street, Suite D
El Segundo, CA 90245
(310) 640-8885

ISBN: 978-0-9996519-9-5

Dedication

I want to thank Suzy and Joan for guiding and encouraging me in the process of writing this book.

I also want to thank my husband, Matthew and our daughter Ann for pointing out the strengths, skills and talents I have and for believing in me.

Stop by our Itty Bitty® Publishing website to find out more about Stress Reduction

www.IttyBittyPublishing.com

Or visit Denise Thomson at

dythomson@gmail.com

Table of Contents

Step 1. What is Stress?
Step 2. How Does Stress Affect Relationships?
Step 3. How Does Stress Affect Health?
Step 4. How Does Stress Affect Business?
Step 5. How Does Stress Affect Weight?
Step 6. How Does Stress Affect Children?
Step 7. How Does Stress Affect Your Brain?
Step 8. How Does Money Affect Stress?
Step 9. How Does Stress Affect Marriage?
Step 10. How Does Stress Affect Learning And Education?
Step 11. How Does Stress Affect Your Values?
Step 12. How Does Stress Affect Your Authenticity?
Step 13. How Does Stress Affect Your Sleep?
Step 14. How Does Stress Affect Harmony In Your Life?
Step 15. How Does Stress Increase Disease?

Introduction

In this book, I am sharing information from my experiences as a nurse and health practitioner that will help you recognize and reduce the stress in your life.

I want to give you hope. Use this information to reduce your stress and become healthier and happier.

Step 1
What Is Stress?

Signs of stress can be physical, mental or emotional. Stress can result in tension in your body, stomach aches, headaches, shoulder aches, injuries and illness. Stress can result in depression. Stress is a reaction to the situations in which you find yourself. It's your mind and body's way of responding to negative thoughts, emotions and situations.

1. Physical stress occurs through exertion. It generally results in pain or stiffness.
2. Mental stress surfaces when your brain is in overload.
3. Emotional stress happens when you are not in control of your circumstances.

Stress can impact your health and your effectiveness. Stress:

   a. Causes injury.
   b. Leads to depression.
   c. Can result in chronic disease.

Signs of Stress (Just To Mention A Few)

- Headaches
- Too little or too much sleep
- Feeling anxious or lethargic
- Depression
- Indigestion

10 Natural Ways to Lower Stress:

- Learn simple meditation techniques, which can include guided imagery.
- Begin to recognize when you're holding onto stress in your body.
- Take a short walk outside, if possible.
- If you're at work, walk away from your desk for a few minutes.
- Listen to some calming music.
- Watch a favorite comedy movie.
- Talk to a good friend.
- Try to exercise regularly or do some stretching.
- If possible, take a short nap.
- Spend some time with your pet(s).

Step 2
How Does Stress Affect Relationships?

People who are stressed have less patience, understanding and tolerance, which can result in friction in your relationship.

1. Decide on an agreed upon time to talk about the stress affecting your relationship. Keep judgment out of the room.
2. Always resolve issues before going to bed.
3. Take time out of your busy schedule first for yourself, then with your loved one(s).
4. Tension increases when not taken care of. Be in charge of your life and reduce stress whenever possible.
5. Prevention is a good way to avoid too much stress. Do something you enjoy to change your thought process.

Signs of Stress-Affected Relationships

Recognizing the signs of stress is the first step to reducing or avoiding negative outcomes.

- Fighting verbally or physically.
- Lack of tolerance for each other.
- Impatience.
- Distancing from each other.
- Negativity.
- Breaking off the relationship.
- Avoidance of issues.
- Needing to be right.

Step 3
How Does Stress Affect Your Health?

Stress costs American industry more than $300 billion annually (OSHA), a stress factor in itself. Stress releases cortisol in your body which:

1. Raises blood pressure
2. Elevates blood sugar
3. Causes tension in your body
4. Brings about headaches
5. Clogs arteries
6. Sets off difficulty in breathing
7. Produces weight gain
8. Results in unpleasant behavior
9. Causes disease(s)

Tips on How to Reduce Stress

- Using guided imagery is helpful in lowering your cortisol levels.
- Reduce stress and its side effects by
  - exercising daily,
  - gardening
  - eating healthy, nutritious meals,
  - drinking 8-10 glasses of water a day,
  - making sure to get the proper amount of sleep. Hours slept before midnight count as double and are more important than hours slept after midnight.

Step 4
How Does Stress Affect Your Business?

When stressed out, your output of work and your behavior can show it. Your work may not be up to par, often due to a lack of concentration. In some cases, this can lead to dismissal from your job, which causes even more stress.

1. Stress keeps you from focusing.
2. Stress makes you nervous.
3. Stress makes you sick.
4. Stress pushes you away from other coworkers, family and friends.
5. Stress interferes with your work performance.
6. Stress only feeds on itself.

Tips On How to Avoid Being Affected By Stress

Most tips are easy to follow:

- Take regular breaks.
- Do breathing exercises.
- Drink water regularly during the day.
- Get 6-8 hours of sleep a night.
- Meditate to relax.
- Communicate regularly to avoid miscommunication.

Step 5
How Does Stress Affect Your Weight?

Stress causes the cortisol level in your body to rise, which increases weight gain. Although it's easy to raise your cortisol level, meditating for five minutes will reduce cortisol, and elevate serotonin and adrenalin. Stress may also go to the other extreme, causing a loss of appetite, which can also lead to poor health.

1. Stress increases snacking.
2. Comfort foods result in weight gain.
3. Eating right before bedtime can cause digestion problems, agitation or sleeplessness. Enjoy your last light bite 1 - 2 hours before going to bed.
4. If depression is added to the mix, lack of exercise can become an issue.

Tips on How to Avoid Weight Gain Due To Stress

- Get up, walk, stretch, avoid elevators and escalators when possible.
- Park away from your building, walk and use the time to mentally prepare for the day.
- Wear good walking shoes; put on the high heels when you arrive at your destination.
- Take regular bathroom breaks; do not hold it, as this causes bladder infections, pain, stress.
- Eat fewer calories than you burn to release pounds.
- Avoid dehydration by drinking 8-10 glasses of water a day.

Step 6
How Does Stress Affect Children?

Stress affects different children in different ways.

It's essential to try and alleviate your stress before you interact with your children. While that isn't always possible, it's important to be aware of the long-term damage you can inflict on your kids when the atmosphere in your house is filled with constant anxiety.

1. Children respond in different ways to continual stress coming from their parents that can include either acting out or keeping their distressed feelings bottled up.
2. These can lead to sleep or eating disorders (which can lead to lethargy), as well as problems at school.
3. Make a concentrated effort to calm down while you are heading home from work.
4. Teach your children to give you five or ten minutes before they begin telling you what they need when you first walk in the door. It will help you diffuse from the day.

How to Prevent Children From Being Affected By Stress.

Here are some suggestions for reducing stress in your own life and your life with your children.

- Take time to play with your children.
- Go on walks or bike rides.
- Encourage them to help you in anything you do. Tell them, show them, supervise them.
- Encourage them to ask questions.
- Take them seriously; make the effort to really listen to them.
- Do not ignore them.
- Be careful not to lecture and judge.

Step 7
How Does Stress Affect Your Brain?

When you are stressed out, you lack focus while at work. You get confused and cannot perform your tasks. You get headaches that increase in intensity the more stressed you are, which can lead to a brain aneurysm, a stroke or some other disease.

1. Taking pills for headaches is only masking the symptoms. Zeroing in on the cause of your headache takes care of the root issue.
2. Stress can cause dehydration, which affects the brain and causes headaches. Drink water every hour during the day.
3. Taking a 5-minute break, stretching, taking a bathroom break, or just moving around, lessens stress and makes you feel better.
4. Shifting your thoughts to something positive and fun reduces stress.
5. Using a game strategy to solve a problem is helpful in releasing stress.
6. Find the fun in what you do.

Tips to Reduce Stress Affecting Your Brain

This is a conscious choice on your part. You can choose to reduce stress or to keep on living with it.

- Altitude changes increase pressure in your ears, which causes stress due to pain, then affects the brain. Chewing gum or yawning reduces pressure and pain.
- Overloading your brain with information can cause confusion and an inability to think clearly.
- When stress affects your brain, it also affects your body.

Step 8
How Does Money Affect Stress?

There's an old adage which claims that having a lot of money doesn't make you happy. Most people who are trying to stretch a tiny paycheck every two weeks will most certainly roll their eyes at that idea. Having a car that needs work, worrying about school needs for the kids, medical bills or sometimes worst of all – feeling terror about how you're going to feed your family when there's next to nothing left after paying rent, electric, etc. – the stress levels a parent feels can be off the map. It's essential that you look at the situation in the cold light of day and make the changes that need to be made.

1. Was money an issue when you were a child? It's a good bet that those attitudes will continue during your adult years.
2. It helps to make a detailed budget in order to make changes that will lighten the load.
3. Decide if you can live with just the bare necessities for a time until you can create a more balanced financial picture.
4. Consider finding a different job that might be better for your stress levels.
5. Meditation is *essential* in this situation.

More Ideas to Consider For Reducing Stress Over Finances

After creating an airtight budget:

- Build an emergency fund. Put a few dollars away towards an emergency from every paycheck.
- Keep your funds separate:
  - Emergency fund
  - Investment fund
  - Retirement fund
  - Vacation fund

If the kids are old enough, they can help. Just the little bit they bring in might be enough to buy that new game or toy they've been wanting. More importantly, it teaches them the value of money at a young age and how to handle it. They can:

- Mow a neighbor's lawn
- Collect recyclables
- Raise vegetables to sell at a Farmer's Markets
- Have a paper route
- Sell home made lemonade at a stand

With everyone pitching in, endless worry over finances will be alleviated.

Step 9
How Does Stress Affect Your Marriage?

Stress in a marriage can cause tension, friction, dissatisfaction, lack of communication. It can even create a hostile environment. People often don't realize that these symptoms are stress-related and that they need to be addressed. The more stress one of the partners is experiencing, the more tension is created between the two people or within the entire family.

1. Stress creates unnecessary issues to surface as things are said that are neither meant nor relevant to the situation.
2. Most people get stressed because they do not like hearing what is said about them.
3. Learn from a new situation without fretting over it.

Ways to Avoid Stress Affecting Your Marriage

When you realize that your relationship is getting tense, seek counseling for you and your spouse. A trained professional, in a neutral environment, can help both of you reduce stress.

- Spend more time together.
- Be open and honest. Talk about everything that concerns both of you.
- Relax together. Watch funny or romantic movies. Go for a walk.
- No secrets. They only cause doubt, which causes trouble, stress and divorce.
- Never speak out of anger, stress or frustration. Take a deep breath, think, and, when you have something constructive to say – then speak.

Step 10
How Does Stress Affect Learning and Education?

The best learning/education happens in a relaxed, calm atmosphere, without stress. Stress is counter-productive to learning. There are different learning styles; find the one(s) that fit you best.

1. Kinesthetic, Visual and Auditory are three of the most common ones. Everyone has usually all three within them; however, at a different percentage for each. The one style that rates the highest percentage is the dominant learning style, followed by the next one and then the lowest one.
2. There are ways to improve learning by adapting to the learning styles.
3. When a subject is taught in a non-dominant way, have someone from the class or team repeat it in their own words until you get it.
4. Speak up when you don't get it! Not speaking up creates stress.
5. As a teacher, to avoid stress, teach in all three combinations, so every student gets something out of the lesson.

How Stress Affects Your Learning and Education

Sometimes, the synapses in the brain fire too fast or too slowly to comprehend what's being taught. When you cannot figure out why you are having trouble learning or studying, go see a professional therapist who can help you reduce stress to learn faster.

- The mind is occupied with stress and cannot process the information received.
- Stress closes the mind, hindering the brain from absorbing the information taught.

Tips To Avoid Stress from Affecting Your Learning And Education

- Take regular breaks, move around, take deep breaths and relax for a couple of minutes.
- Make sure you stay hydrated with water.
- When questions arise that you cannot answer in a reasonable time frame, ASK for help.

Step 11
How Does Stress Affect Value in Your Life?

People have a tendency to devalue themselves when they are stressed out, as they cannot see their own strengths. This is not a productive way of living a good life. Stay strong, don't let anyone doubt your values and all you have to offer. You have a reason to be where you are and that alone has value.

1. Value yourself. Be true, honest and authentic with yourself and others.
2. Recognize your values and use them to their fullest. Others will appreciate you for who you are when you stand firm and true.
3. Appreciate your values. You don't need to brag; just allow yourself to accept them.
4. Share your values with others who want to know. By sharing, you strengthen your own values.
5. Most importantly, try to be diligent in recognizing the amount of stress you are experiencing and how it affects your level of self-esteem, (as well as your body).

Signs That Your Values Are Affected By Stress

Hints that you devalue yourself are usually pointed out by loved ones asking you: "Why are you putting yourself down?"

- Stress causes you to diminish the values in your life.
- Stress can be very powerful and destructive as to how you see yourself, physically and mentally.

Ways to Avoid Allowing Stress To Affect Your Value.

- Be aware of how stress can exacerbate feelings of a lack of self-worth.
- Do not give in to stress. Take a break, hydrate, breathe deeply, exercise and remind yourself that you are doing your best.

Step 12
How Does Stress Affect Your Authenticity?

Be your true self. Be in control of yourself and do not let others influence you negatively. Stand up for what you believe. Stay away from the naysayers.

1. Stress wears you down. Do not cave in to outside negative influences.
2. Stress is destructive and can cause acting out or severe depression.
3. When people attack you, it makes you question what you believe and who you are as a person, which often causes a large amount of stress. If it's a particularly vulnerable time in your life, you can begin to believe their opinions about you – and your stress and depression only escalate.
4. Be authentic no matter what. It helps to center yourself as often as you can with relaxation techniques such as meditation.

Tips on How to Live In Your Authenticity

Living in your authenticity. Is that tough for you? What's holding you back from being authentic? Have you had experiences where you allowed your authenticity to be compromised? Stress plays a big part in one's inability to live an authentic life. Self-hatred can destroy a person's self-esteem and lead to a never-ending cycle of worry and stress. My tip is: Be strong, be authentic, and live life to its fullest!

- Surround yourself with positive and relaxed people.
- Stay away from people who attack your authenticity.
- Always remain true to yourself.

Step 13
How Does Stress Affect Sleep?

Stress affects your deep sleep. It prevents you from being relaxed in the morning when you wake up. Getting up during the night, groggy, irritated in the morning, not wanting to get out of bed? 7 out of 10 adults in the USA experience stress daily.

1. Sleep-deprived people are more likely to be stressed out.
2. Science has found that every hour slept before midnight counts twice as much as the hours slept after midnight.
3. Avoid stimulating your brain synapses to fire at a high rate before going to bed.
4. Do deep breathing or stretching, to calm you down before going to bed, so you can fall asleep quickly and deeply.

Tips On How to Sleep Better and Not Be Affected By Stress

Stress does not allow for deep and relaxing sleep. It robs you of the hours you need to rejuvenate your brain, your body. Once again, every hour slept before midnight counts as double time; whereas the hours slept after midnight are not that deep with the REM cycle in your sleep. Not sleeping well can also be due to sleep apnea, where you stop breathing for a short time, as your glottal tissue covers up the wind pipe. If you're experiencing this, get tested for sleep apnea.

- The CPAP helps you sleep deeper, and allows relaxed waking up in the morning.
- Take a hot bath or shower before going to bed. This helps you relax.

- Have a clean and uncluttered bedroom, helping to create a sanctuary for yourself.
- If possible, leave no arguments unresolved before going to bed.

Step 14
How Does Stress Affect Harmony in Your Life?

Harmony in life is so important to your health. Harmony is a weapon towards stress. When you live a life in harmony, you are usually happy, healthy and stress is non-existent.

1. Make the decision to create harmony in your life, wherever possible.
2. Harmony helps you overcome stress.

Tips for Living Life in Harmony

Do whatever it takes for you to relax and de-stress. Listen to music, watch a funny or relaxing movie, read a book, exercise. There are so many ways to live life in harmony; choose the way that works best for you!

- Living in harmony is ultimately your choice.
- Living in harmony means loving yourself.
- A harmonious life has no room for stress.
- Harmony and balance allow for a beautiful life.
- Living harmoniously is peace on earth.
- Benefits of Having Meaning in Life are: Clarity, Focus, Productivity,
- Creativity, Resourcefulness, Drive, Inner Strength, Perseverance.
- Personal Growth, A Meaningful Life

Step 15
How Does Stress Increase Disease?

Stress is defined as an illness that affects a person, animal, or plant. (Webster's Dictionary) 75 – 90% of all doctor's office visits are for stress-related ailments and complaints such as headaches, high blood pressure, heart problems, diabetes, skin conditions, asthma, arthritis, depression and anxiety. OSHA claims that stress in the USA alone costs more than $300 billion annually.

1. Exercise daily to reduce stress.
2. Eat healthy.
3. Hydrate properly.
4. Live a life in harmony and balance.
5. Play relaxing music or spend time with a close friend for help in relieving your stress.
6. Don't dwell on things you cannot change.
7. Yesterday is History, tomorrow is a Mystery, today is a gift – that's why it's called the Present. Live in the present, do, give, and be your best daily!

Tips to Avoid or Reduce Stress-Related Disease

- Choose between stress-causing disease or a happy and relaxed life, increasing health.
- You are in control. Don't allow others to take your control away from you.
- Love yourself. You cannot love yourself and create stress at the same time. Stress is a reflection on how you perceive things or yourself.
- Take care of yourself first; schedule time daily, so you are energized and living in harmony.
- Send stress on its way and fend off disease with harmony, authenticity, being true to yourself.

You've finished. Before you go...

Tweet/share that you finished this book.

Please star rate this book.

Reviews are solid gold to writers. Please take a few minutes to give us some itty bitty feedback.

ABOUT THE AUTHOR

Denise Y Thomson has over 40 years experience in nursing, teaching, coaching health and wellness and grief counseling.

While attending a private college and receiving her certification in business (while also serving as the school nurse), Denise saved two lives by recognizing the signs of blood poisoning. She urged the school administrator to take the first student to the doctor immediately and stood her ground until the administrator called the doctor and took the student there. According to the doctor, the student had maybe a few more days to live, had he not come in right then for treatment. When another student complained that she could not raise her arm, Denise saw the red line again and insisted that this student had to go see the doctor in town immediately. Without much resistance this time, the doctor was seen and this time the student only had a matter of hours to live. Both times, Denise made the correct call, and both students lived because of the treatment.

During all these years, Denise learned a few things in practical applications. She has her LVN certification, FTC, BA in Linguistics, MAED. She also taught CPR classes for the American Heart Association, as well as for the American Red Cross and is also certified as Health and Wellness Coach.

Denise Y Thomson enjoys working with people, sharing her tools to help them live a happy, healthy and balanced life. Her passion is sharing and educating people and making a difference in this world.

Disclaimer: I am not a medical doctor; therefore, these are experiences and suggestions I am sharing with you. Please check with your doctor before doing anything that could harm you.

dythomson@gmail.com

If you liked this Amazing Itty Bitty® Book you might also enjoy…

- **Your Amazing Itty Bitty Heal Your Body Book** – Patricia Garza Pinto
- **Your Amazing Itty Bitty® Diet FREE Weight Loss Book** – Liz Bull
- **Your Amazing Itty Bitty® Weight Loss Book** – Suzy Prudden and Joan Meijer

Or any of our many Itty Bitty® Books available on line.

www.ingramcontent.com/pod-product-compliance
Lightning Source LLC
Chambersburg PA
CBHW061305040426
42444CB00010B/2521